Warnings!

Before you start:

1. **Cover your work area with newspapers or craft paper!** Making jewelry can get messy.

2. **Get a parent's permission to make the jewelry projects!** Better yet, have him or her help you! It's a lot of fun to make this fantastic jewelry with a parent.

3. **Clean up afterward!** If you want to make crafts again, make sure you clean up your mess!

4. **Recycle what you can from your projects!** Old shoeboxes work great for storing possible jewelry doodads for future projects.

5. **Read through all of the instructions before starting a project.**

Things you'll need

- ❋ scissors
- ❋ jewelry findings
- ❋ jewelry pliers
- ❋ lobster clasps (from this kit)
- ❋ old buttons
- ❋ toothpicks
- ❋ egg carton
- ❋ ruler
- ❋ glue
- ❋ magazines & newspapers

Where to shop

Find some of the items you need at home. Most likely, you'll have to go on a treasure hunt at thrift stores, dollar stores, garage sales, and flea markets to find exactly what you want. You shouldn't spend too much money on any object that you buy. And definitely don't buy new, except for the jewelry findings, which you can find at craft stores. This is all about recycling!

This necklace was made using recycled beads from old necklaces, bracelets, and earrings found at garage sales.

- ❊ old jewelry
- ❊ leather string, elastic string, or embroidery floss
- ❊ earring hooks
- ❊ lobster clasp or old buttons (for the fastener)
- ❊ jump rings

Old Jewelry Redux

Out of every $10 you spend buying something, $1 goes into the packaging. So, why buy new with all that packaging when you can reuse your tired old jewelry? Or maybe save a necklace or bracelet from a garage sale. This is the easiest and least expensive way to make recycled jewelry!

Get a parent's permission to use the old jewelry! And don't take apart antique jewelry!

Make your own Recycled Jewelry

Written by Heather Dakota and Nancy Panaccione
Illustrated and designed by Nancy Panaccione

an imprint of
SCHOLASTIC
www.scholastic.com

Scholastic and Tangerine Press and associated logos are trademarks and/or registered trademarks of Scholastic Inc.

Published by Tangerine Press, an imprint of Scholastic Inc., 557 Broadway; New York, NY 10012

10 9 8 7 6 5 4 3 2 1

ISBN: 978-0-545-23522-8

Scholastic Canada Ltd.; Markham, Ontario
Scholastic Australia Pty. Ltd; Gosford NSW
Scholastic New Zealand Ltd.; Greenmount, Auckland

jewelry is super-fun to wear!

It is very important to reduce, reuse, and recycle as much as you can. Did you know that the US is the number one trash-producing country in the world? Each person produces 1,609 pounds (729 kg) of garbage each year! But you can turn trash into treasures by making recycled jewelry. Let's recycle!

Table of Contents

Old Jewelry Redux.. 4

Plastic Bottle Earrings................................ 6

Magazine Bead Bracelet........................... 8

Comic Book Bracelet................................ 14

Bottle Cap Barrette and Necklace Set.... 18

Pop-top Bracelet 22

"It's a Wrap" Bracelet 26

Found-object Pendant 30

WHAT YOU DO:

1 Unstring an old necklace or bracelet.

2 Arrange the beads in the order that you want them.

3 Slide the beads over your string of choice. Make the string as long as you need for a bracelet or necklace.

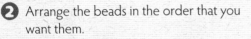

4 Tie on a lobster clasp if you're making a bracelet or necklace. Or, add the beads to an earring finding.

If you run out of lobster clasps, use a button as your fastener. See P.13 for instructions.

OLD JEWELRY MADE NEW!

Pieces found at garage sales.

PARENT'S
HELP
NEEDED!

Plastic Bottle Earrings

A plastic bottle takes 700 years before it will even begin to decompose. That makes for a lot of plastic bottles in landfills. Before throwing out your next bottle, think about making some funky earrings instead!

WHAT YOU DO:

1. Thoroughly wash the plastic container with hot water and soap. Let it dry overnight.

2. Cut the plastic bottle into pieces and in whatever shape you want (like a triangle, circle, square, spiral, or rectangle).

3. Use only one piece or arrange the different shapes together.

4. Punch a hole in the top of each piece and slide the pieces onto the earring hook.

To create a spiral, first cut a circle. Then, cut into the circle about ¼ in. (6.5 mm) from the edge. Keep cutting around and around, smaller and smaller, until you reach the center of the circle.

DON'T HAVE PIERCED EARS?
No worries! Turn your cool earring designs into a pendant for you and your BFF!

* magazines
* ruler
* glue
* scissors
* toothpick or coffee stirrer
* elastic string or embroidery floss
* lobster clasp or button
* empty egg carton

Magazine Bead Bracelet

We could save about 250 million trees each year if every American recycled his or her newspapers and magazines. Start recycling by making some super-fly jewelry using your favorite magazine!

Parent's Permission Needed

8

making the Beads

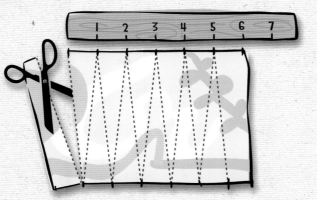

1. Use the ruler to mark off the length of the bead you want to make. We used 1 in. (2.5 cm) for the base of this bead.

2. On the opposite side of the length of the magazine page, start your marks on the half-in. (1.3 cm) mark. Then, mark off every inch (2.5 cm).

3. Cut from one mark to the other side making a triangle.

making the beads [continued]

4 Starting at the base of the triangle, roll the magazine cutting around the toothpick or coffee stirrer. Make sure it's tight and centered.

5 When you get to the skinny end of your triangle, put a dab of glue on the tail. Finish wrapping the end.

HINT:
If glue comes out of the sides, don't worry! Just keep wrapping and spreading the glue around the outside of your bead.

6 Set the bead and toothpick into an old egg carton to dry overnight.

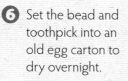

STRING THE BRACELET

1 Carefully pull your beads off of the toothpick. They should have a nice round hole going through the center.

2 Cut a 10-in. (25-cm) length of your string.

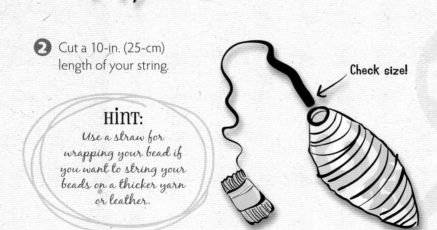

Check size!

HINT:
Use a straw for wrapping your bead if you want to string your beads on a thicker yarn or leather.

STRING THE BRACELET [continued]

3 Thread as many beads as you'd like onto the string.

4 Check the size on your arm before tying the ends together. The beads should fit around your wrist but should not be tight.

TRY THIS!

Use different kinds of paper for your beads, like newspaper, gift wrap, brown paper bags, scrapbooking paper, catalogs, junk mail, or colored copy paper.

finishing your Bracelet

5 If you used elastic string for your bracelet, tie a knot with the two string ends. Make another knot so it is secure. The knot will disappear into the beads. The bracelet should easily slip on and off of your wrist.

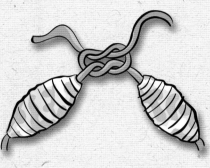

6 If you are using yarn or other non-stretchy material, tie on the lobster clasp. If you have run out of lobster clasps, use an old button. (See button clasp instructions to the right.)

Create a button clasp

Tie a button on one end of your bracelet or necklace. Use a button that coordinates with the jewelry you're making.

On the other end of your jewelry piece, knot a loop in your string that is just large enough for the button to go through.

gather it up!

* old comic books
* small round beads
* elastic cording or other stretchy string material
* scissors
* glue
* toothpicks
* egg carton

Comic Book Bracelet

US paper recycling has saved more than 90 million cubic yards of landfill space. You can help by not throwing out your old comic books. Instead, make some really cool comic book bracelets!

Parent's Permission Needed

Making the Beads

Roll the beads the same way you did for the Magazine Bead Bracelet (P. 8). If you want to get creative, turn to P. 17 to see how to cut the paper to make different bead shapes.

String the Beads

1 Lay out your beads in the order you want them strung.

2 Cut your elastic cord to roughly 36 in. (91 cm) long. String on a round bead, one of your recycled beads, and then another round bead. The three beads should be in the center of your cord.

string the beads [continued]

3 Now, pick up a recycled bead, and thread both ends of the cord through opposite sides of the bead. Pull gently to tighten the beads close together.

4 Add one round bead to each end. Pick up another recycled bead and pass both ends through the bead and pull gently to tighten. Repeat until you have added enough beads for the chain to go comfortably around your wrist.

5 When the bracelet is the right length, add a final round bead to each end of the string. Bring one of the ends of the cord back through the first recycled bead. Tie a secure knot. Congratulations! You did it!

Bead Variations:

Tired of making the same shaped beads over and over? Need a bit of variety? Try these really cool ways of cutting your paper to make a different style of bead!

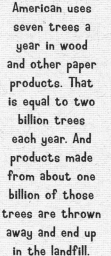

* clean bottle caps
* old barrette
* felt or wide ribbon
* button or lobster clasp
* glue
* magazines
* stickers
* glitter glue
* scissors

Bottle Cap Barrette and Necklace Set

Long ago, aluminum was more valuable than gold. So, let's put that value into a barrette and necklace set. Go through your hair doodads. Does one need a makeover? Perfect! Did you just finish a soda with a bottle cap? Great! It's time to get down to some recycling!

Parent's Permission Required!

THE BOTTLE CAP BARRETTE

1 Decorate the inside of the bottle caps with magazine pictures, small found objects, and glitter glue. Secure your decorations to the inside of the bottle cap with glue and let dry.

2 When your bottle caps are decorated, fill the inside of the cap with a liquid glue that dries clear.

3 Once dry, put strong glue on the backs of the bottle caps and press them firmly to the barrette. You may have to hold them in place until the glue dries a bit.

4 **DO NOT put this in your hair right away!** Let it dry overnight.

♲ FACT:

Americans consume more than 80 billion cans of soda every year. Thanks to recycling, less than one percent goes into the landfills.

Bottle Cap Necklace

When an aluminum can is thrown away, it will still be there in 500 years. And maybe 500 years from now your descendants will still be wearing this stylin' necklace made from recycled bottle caps and old buttons.

Making the Necklace

1. Just like you did for the barrette, clean, decorate, and seal your bottle caps with glue.

2. Cut a strip of felt long enough to go around your neck with 1 in. (2.5 cm) of overlap. Sew a button onto one end of the felt. On the other end of the felt, cut a slit just big enough for the button.

3. Arrange the bottle caps on the felt strip. Squeeze glue onto the back of each bottle cap and stick them to the felt.

4. Make sure you don't move the necklace until it is completely dry.

gather it up!

* 7 soda can pop tops
* ribbon
* scissors
* lobster clasp
* glue
* nail file
* needle and thread (optional)

Pop-top Bracelet

Aluminum beverage cans are the most recycled item in the US. Other aluminum pieces can be recycled, too! Pop tops are aluminum. This awesome pop-top bracelet is a great way to recycle. And, it's stylish, too!

Be careful! The edge that comes off the can is sharp. It will be covered by your ribbon though!

WHAT YOU DO:

1 Gather your pop tops and carefully file off any sharp edges using a nail file. The ribbon will cover the edges.

2 Cut a piece of ribbon 5 in. (13 cm) long. This will make a 6-in. (15-cm) bracelet when finished, so adjust the size to fit your wrist.

3 String five of the pop tops onto the ribbon by threading the ribbon up through one pop top opening and down through the next.

This is how it will look with all five pop tops in place.

♻ **FACT:**

More aluminum goes into a beverage can than any other product. But there is no limit to the number of times the aluminum can be recycled!

Recycling one aluminum can saves enough energy to run a TV for three hours.

④ Flip the entire ribbon with pop tops over so you can see the back.

⑤ Take one of the two remaining pop tops, and add it to one end of the ribbon, bringing the ribbon up through just one opening of the pop top and fold the ribbon back onto itself. (**Note:** This covers the sharp edges.)

⑥ Do the same on the other end.

7 Glue both ribbon ends down, making a loop. You may need to hold the ribbon together until the glue sets. Let dry completely before continuing.

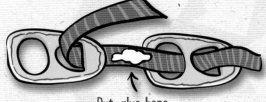

Put glue here

(You can also sew the ribbon ends closed.)

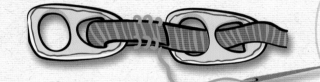

Remember!
Have a parent help you with the needle and thread if you sew your ribbon closed.

8 Attach a lobster clasp and wear your new earth-friendly creation proudly.

✳ 30-35 clean
candy wrappers
(any kind of wrappers
will work)

FUN FACT:
The average American
consumes 21 lbs.
(9.5 kg) of candy
each year.

"It's a Wrap" Bracelet

You love jewelry. And you love the planet.

Here's a great way to save the planet

and make a sweet bracelet!

WHAT YOU DO:

1 Fold the long side of the candy wrapper toward the center.

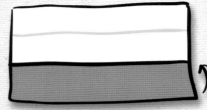

2 Do the same thing to the other side.

3 Fold the candy wrapper in half lengthwise.

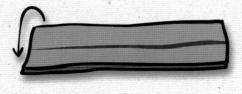

4 Fold the candy wrapper in half lengthwise, again.

WHAT YOU DO: (continued)

5 Fold the wrapper in half. Open it back up.

 FACT:

Not many people realize that you can recycle the aluminum wrapper from a Hershey's® kiss®. Eighty million kisses are wrapped each day. That's the same as 40 football fields of aluminum.

6 Fold the ends in toward the center fold and then fold in half.

7 Follow Steps 1-6 with another wrapper.

8 Insert the ends of the first wrapper through the folded end of the second wrapper and pull through.

9 Continue folding wrappers and adding links.

10 When the bracelet is big enough to fit over your hand, you're ready to add the last link. Fold the last link as you did the others, but unfold the ends before inserting into the previous link.

11 Bend the bracelet into a circle. Wrap the loose ends over and through the first link.

- ✳ plastic lid from a wide-mouth jar, or other plastic lid
- ✳ small objects, like plastic toys, Scrabble® letters, Monopoly® pieces, flowers, or keys (These need to be able to fit in the jar lid.)
- ✳ photocopy of a favorite photo or background image
- ✳ ribbon scrap
- ✳ wire or jewelry finding
- ✳ scissors
- ✳ glue

Found-object Pendant

Do you have a junk drawer of all kinds of stuff? Are your board games missing some pieces? Why not combine a bunch of little items into a one-of-a-kind pendant that tells the world all about you!

warning!
You'll need your parent's permission to use the found objects. And you'll need help making a hole in the lid.

WHAT YOU DO:

1. Gather all your found objects and arrange them in the jar lid the way you want them. Don't forget where they go!

2. Use the scissors to make a hole in the center top of the rim. If you're having trouble, ask a parent for help.

3. Cut your background image to fit inside the lid.

4. Glue your photo or background image to the inside of the lid. Make sure the hole is at the top, so your image is right-side up and not tilted.

5. Start layering your found objects the way you want them. Put a dab of glue on the back of the object and stick it onto the background.

6. When everything is dry, use a jewelry finding or wire to make a hook for attaching the ribbon. Slide the pendant onto the ribbon and tie a secure knot. Beautiful!

Make Earrings!

Use smaller plastic caps and earring hooks to create one-of-a-kind recycled earrings. Find small pictures for your jewelry in magazines and newspapers.

WOW!

You've just saved a bunch of junk from going into the landfill. And not only that, but you made some super-cool jewelry, too! Keep your imagination going and see what else you can make from stuff you find around the house, at garage sales, or even flea markets. You may even be able to start your very own recycled jewelry business!

It costs about $30 per ton to recycle trash, $50 to send it to the landfill, and $65 to $75 to burn it. But, it doesn't cost much at all to make jewelry out of it. Which would you rather do?

HAPPY RECYCLING!